MADAGASCAR 2016 HUMAN RIGHTS REPORT

EXECUTIVE SUMMARY

Madagascar is a constitutional democracy with a popularly elected president, a bicameral legislature (Senate and National Assembly), prime minister, and cabinet. The current president and National Assembly were elected in 2013, the first national elections after the 2009 coup against former president Ravalomanana. Nationwide municipal elections in July 2015 allowed for the indirect election of the Senate in December 2015. All elections were peaceful and deemed generally free and fair by international observers, despite low turnout and the denial of 31 of 31 opposition appeals by the High Constitutional Court.

Civilian authorities at times did not maintain effective control over the security forces.

The most important human rights abuses included the inability of the government to provide rule of law, which resulted in official corruption and impunity, as well as security force abuse; increased restrictions on freedoms of speech, press, and assembly; and child labor, including forced child labor.

Other human rights problems included unlawful killings; life-threatening prison conditions; lack of judicial independence and judicial inefficiency, resulting in lengthy pretrial detention; societal discrimination and violence against women; child abuse and child marriage; discrimination against persons with disabilities and members of the lesbian, gay, bisexual, transgender, and intersex (LGBTI) community; mob violence; and trafficking in persons.

The government rarely prosecuted or punished officials who committed abuses, whether in the security forces or elsewhere in the government, and impunity remained a problem.

Section 1. Respect for the Integrity of the Person, Including Freedom from:

a. Arbitrary Deprivation of Life and other Unlawful or Politically Motivated Killings

There were numerous reports the government or its agents committed arbitrary or unlawful killings of criminal suspects. Most killings occurred during security force operations to stem cattle rustling by armed criminal groups in the central, west, and southwest areas of the country. Villagers sometimes supported government efforts to stem cattle rustling and were responsible for killing cattle rustlers; sometimes they opposed security forces or one another.

In January a National Gendarmerie report stated gendarmes had killed 36 presumed thieves in 2015. This figure did not include those killed during Operation Fahalemana, a joint security forces operation to reestablish government control in the 11 regions where cattle rustlers were the most active and violent. Government forces reportedly killed hundreds of presumed cattle thieves during that operation, which officially ended in December 2015. Killings of presumed cattle thieves continued through this year. Although officials promised to investigate several alleged retaliatory executions in 2015, no outcomes of any such investigation were made public. During the year media implicated security forces in at least 199 deaths in armed confrontations, mainly with suspected cattle thieves. Media reports also implicated security forces in the deaths of other security force members and occasionally of innocent villagers. In June a total of 23 persons were killed in a confrontation with security forces, including 18 thieves and five villagers, after a gang of 80 thieves allegedly attacked the village and stole 100 cattle.

b. Disappearance

In February a miner in the southern region of Anjozorobe, identified as Mandignisoa, disappeared after a confrontation with two gendarmes linked to the Presidential Guard. Media, family members, and local protesters asserted he had been killed by shots fired by one of the gendarmes. The body of the alleged victim was not recovered, although at the end of March, his family stated the matter was resolved. The chief of the gendarmerie of Antananarivo claimed no killing had taken place, and there was no report of a government investigation into the alleged shooting.

c. Torture and Other Cruel, Inhuman, or Degrading Treatment or Punishment

The constitution and law provide for the inviolability of the person and prohibit such practices, but security forces subjected prisoners and criminal suspects to physical and mental abuse, including torture, according to nongovernmental organizations (NGOs) and media reports.

Security personnel used beatings as punishment for alleged crimes or as a means of coercion. Off-duty and sometimes intoxicated members of the armed forces assaulted civilians. In most cases investigations announced by security officials did not result in prosecutions. For example, on March 6, an intoxicated security force member shot and killed a presumed pickpocket in Depot Manangareza Anjoma in Toamasina. The security force member reportedly assaulted the alleged pickpocket in a restaurant and then fired when the individual attempted to escape.

In follow-up to the investigation of the 2015 arrest of student movement leader Jean Pierre Randrianamboarina, the gendarmerie recognized excessive use of force by some of its members and referred the case for a judicial investigation that ended on February 4 with disciplinary sanctions against several officers. No information was available regarding the specific sanctions applied.

The government arrested and imprisoned a few security force members during the year. On May 14, a police inspector was arrested for drug possession after gendarmes found five bags of marijuana in his car. On July 20, a police officer was among nine persons arrested for involvement in a series of kidnappings in Antananarivo.

On August 6, the Court of Antananarivo committed a police officer from the "Service Antigang" unit to the high security prison of Tsiafahy after the officer was suspected of being involved in a holdup in Ampanefy, a locality in southwestern Antananarivo under gendarmerie jurisdiction. The media reported five other police officers, including one working for the presidency, were investigated in the same incident but were not arrested by the gendarmerie.

In October 2015 a Malagasy gendarme officer serving as part of the UN peacekeeping force in the Democratic Republic of the Congo was accused of sexual exploitation of a domestic employee. A UN investigation was pending at year's end. In June the Ministry of Foreign Affairs reported the officer had been disciplined after an investigation.

Prison and Detention Center Conditions

Prison conditions were harsh and life threatening due to inadequate food, overcrowding, poor sanitary conditions, and lack of medical care.

<u>Physical Conditions</u>: As of September, the country's 82 prisons and detention centers held nearly 20,000 inmates, including 860 women, 634 boys, and 47 girls;

this figure represented nearly twice the official capacity of 10,355 inmates. Authorities did not always hold juveniles separately from adults, and some preschool-age children shared cells with their incarcerated mothers.

Grandir Dignement (Grow Up with Dignity), an NGO dedicated to the rights of imprisoned youth, identified 714 minor detainees during the year. The NGO estimated that 48 percent of the prisons had separate areas for minors.

Authorities held pretrial detainees with convicted prisoners.

Severe overcrowding due to weaknesses in the judicial system and inadequate prison infrastructure was a serious problem. One penitentiary surpassed its official capacity by nearly eight-fold. Lengthy pretrial detention was pervasive.

According to the International Committee of the Red Cross (ICRC), almost one in two prisoners nationwide suffered from moderate or severe malnutrition. The ICRC treated more than 4,000 prisoners for malnutrition during the year. Each inmate received approximately 10.5 ounces of cassava per day, compared with the recommended 26 ounces. The ICRC reported that, in the first half of 2015, approximately 50 persons died in prison and 27 of these deaths could be linked to malnutrition.

According to a study conducted in 2015 by Handicap International, harsh prison conditions were a source of psychological distress for 66 percent of detainees at three of the country's largest detention facilities: Vatomandry, Toamasina, and Toliary. In a number of documented cases, disease was a direct result of overcrowding, lack of hygiene and medical care, and poor nutrition. According to the study, 92 percent of detainees reported they "often felt hungry." In many cases families and NGOs supplemented the daily rations of prisoners.

The Ministry of Justice recorded 90 deaths in prisons in 2015, none of which was attributed to actions by guards or other staff.

A deteriorating prison infrastructure that often lacked sanitation facilities and potable water resulted in disease and infestations of insects and rodents. Access to medical care was limited, particularly for detainees held at Tsiafahy, the country's high-security detention center. Ventilation, lighting, and temperature control in facilities were either inadequate or nonexistent.

<u>Administration</u>: Prison recordkeeping remained inadequate and poorly coordinated with police and judicial authorities. There was no ombudsman to advocate on behalf of prisoners or detainees. While a formal process exists to submit complaints of inhumane conditions to judicial authorities, few detainees used it due to fear of reprisal. Ministry of Justice officials conducted intermittent inspections of facilities. Officials authorized prisoners and detainees to receive weekly visits from relatives and permitted religious observance. Visits outside the scheduled days were reportedly possible by bribing guards and penitentiary agents. NGOs reported bribes could purchase small privileges, such as allowing family members to bring food for prisoners.

<u>Independent Monitoring</u>: Authorities generally permitted independent monitoring of prison conditions by the ICRC, several local NGOs, and some diplomatic missions. Authorities permitted the ICRC to conduct visits to all main penitentiary facilities and to hold private consultations in accordance with its standard modalities. Authorities also permitted ICRC representatives to visit detainees in pretrial or temporary detention.

<u>Improvements</u>: According to the national coordinator of Grandir Dignement, in 2015, 48 percent of prisons had a separate area for minors, an improvement from 41 percent in 2014. Christian Association for Development of Environmental Action (ACDM), an NGO dedicated to community development, donated sports equipment, musical instruments, and infrastructure assistance to 10 prisons in the south.

On August 22, the government passed a law that reduces the maximum duration of pretrial detention for minor detainees to three months for correctional matters and six months for criminal matters.

d. Arbitrary Arrest or Detention

The constitution and law prohibit arbitrary arrest and detention, but authorities did not always respect these provisions. Authorities arrested persons on vague charges and detained many suspects for long periods without trial.

Role of the Police and Security Apparatus

The national police, under the authority of the Ministry of Public Security, is responsible for maintaining law and order in urban areas. The gendarmerie, under the Ministry of National Defense, is responsible for maintaining law and order in rural areas. Beginning in 2015 the military became increasingly active in rural areas, particularly to maintain order in areas affected by cattle rustling and banditry.

The government did not have effective control over matters relating to rule of law outside the capital. Security forces at times failed to prevent or respond to societal violence, particularly in rural areas.

Government institutions lacked any effective means to monitor, inspect, or investigate alleged abuse by security forces, and impunity was a problem. Victims may lodge complaints in the local court of jurisdiction, although this rarely occurred.

The law gives traditional village institutions authority to protect property and public order. In some rural areas, an informal, community-organized judicial system known as "dina" resolved civil disputes between villagers over such issues as alleged cattle rustling. The dina system sometimes imposed harsh sentences without due process or failed to protect the rights of victims.

The *Ao Raha* newspaper reported four individuals accused of rape avoided prison after reaching an "amicable agreement" with the victim's family in March. The victim was a 12-year-old girl, and two of the suspects also were minors. The incident occurred in the village of Morafeno in the Maevatanana district, approximately 186 miles from Antananarivo. The gendarmerie investigated the case to determine why the four suspects were not prosecuted. A final determination had not been reached by year's end.

Arrest Procedures and Treatment of Detainees

The law requires arrest warrants in all cases except those involving 'hot pursuit' (the apprehension of a suspect during or immediately after a crime is committed), but authorities often detained persons based on accusations only. The law requires authorities to charge or release criminal suspects within 48 hours of arrest, but they often held individuals for significantly longer periods before charging or releasing them. Defendants have a right to counsel, and the law entitled those who could not afford a lawyer to one provided by the state. Many citizens were unaware of this right, and few requested attorneys. Defendants have the right to know the charges against them, but authorities did not always respect this right. Authorities frequently denied bail without justification. Magistrates often resorted to a "mandat de depot" (retaining writ) under which defendants were held in detention for the entire pretrial period. The law limits the duration of pretrial detention and regulates the use of the writ. Regulations limit the duration of pretrial detention, with a theoretical maximum of eight months for criminal cases. Family members generally had access to prisoners, although authorities limited access for prisoners in solitary confinement or those arrested for political reasons.

Senator Rene Lylison, a member of the opposition party MAPAR, encouraged antigovernment protests, including a citywide strike in Antananarivo on May 24. Although his call for a strike was largely ignored, the government accused him of compromising internal state security. Government officials sought his arrest as a case of "hot pursuit" for seven days before reportedly obtaining a warrant. He remained in hiding at year's end. As a senator he is immune from prosecution or arrest except in so-called hot pursuit.

<u>Arbitrary Arrest</u>: Security forces arbitrarily arrested journalists, political opponents, demonstrators, and other civilians.

<u>Pretrial Detention</u>: According to the Ministry of Justice, as of September approximately 59 percent of the prison population was in pretrial detention. Sixty-seven percent of female prisoners and 88 percent of juvenile prisoners were pretrial detainees. Pretrial detention ranged from several days to several years. Poor recordkeeping, an outdated judicial system, insufficient magistrates, and lack of resources contributed to the problem. The length of pretrial detention often exceeded the maximum sentence for the alleged crime.

<u>Detainee's Ability to Challenge Lawfulness of Detention before a Court</u>: The law provides for the defendant's right to lodge an appeal concerning his or her pretrial detention with no specific provision about his or her right to prompt release and compensation. The law states that a defendant must be released immediately if a prosecutor approves a temporary release requested by the defendant.

e. Denial of Fair Public Trial

Although the constitution and law provide for an independent judiciary, the judiciary was susceptible to executive influence at all levels, and corruption remained a serious problem. There were instances in which the outcome of trials appeared predetermined, and authorities did not always enforce court orders. Lack of training, resources, and personnel hampered judicial effectiveness, and case backlogs were "prodigious," according to Freedom House.

The law reserves military courts for trials of military personnel, and they generally follow the procedures of the civil judicial system, except that military jury members must be military officers. Defendants in military cases have access to an appeals process and generally benefit from the same rights available to civilians, although their trials are not public. A civilian magistrate, usually joined by a panel of military officers, presides over military trials.

Trial Procedures

The law provides for a presumption of innocence, but authorities often ignored this right. Defendants have the right to be informed promptly and in detail of the charges against them, and the law provides free interpretation as necessary, from the moment charged through all appeals. Defendants have the right to a fair trial without undue delay. Prolonged incarceration without charge, denial of bail, and postponed hearings were common.

Trials are public, and defendants have the right to legal counsel at every stage of proceedings. Many citizens were unaware of their right to counsel, however, and authorities did not systematically inform them of it. Defendants who did not request or could not afford counsel generally received very limited time to prepare their cases. Defendants have the right to be present at their trials, to receive information regarding the charges against them, to present and confront witnesses, and to present evidence. Authorities generally respected such rights if defendants had legal representation. Defense attorneys have access to government-held evidence, but this right does not extend to defendants without attorneys. Legislation outlining defendants' rights does not specifically refer to the right not to be compelled to testify or not to confess guilt. It does include the right to assistance by another person during the investigation and trial. Defendants have the right to appeal convictions.

According to law, the above rights apply to all defendants, and there were no reports of any groups being denied any of these rights.

Political Prisoners and Detainees

On August 3, Alain Ramaroson, leader of an opposition party, was arrested and accused of forgery in a land dispute with one of his family members. Ramaroson, who was 62 and in poor health, was held with other prisoners in the same poor conditions that predominated throughout the country's prisons. His attorney requested temporary release, but at year's end it had not been granted. The media reported the Ministry of Justice was blocking his temporary release by keeping his case file for examination. The media also reported he was not allowed to receive visitors without approval of the ministry.

On December 9, Augustin Andriamananoro, vice president of the political party associated with Andry Rajoelina, who served as de facto president for five years after ousting his predecessor in a coup, was arrested during a funeral. He had called for the resignation of President Rajaonarimampianina in July. He was charged with threatening state security and participating in unauthorized demonstrations against Chinese gold mining operations in Soamahamanina between June and November. On November 4, the five alleged leaders of the demonstrations were given one-year suspended sentences, and the case was considered closed until the new arrest in December. Andriamananoro was released on December 27 with a three-month suspended sentence. While in custody, he was given the same protections and rights as other prisoners and was reportedly visited by members of his political party and by the French ambassador. Andriamananoro has dual Malagasy and French citizenship.

Civil Judicial Procedures and Remedies

The judiciary deals with all civil matters, including human rights cases, and individuals or organizations may seek civil remedies for human rights violations. Courts lacked independence, were subject to influence, and often encountered difficulty in enforcing civil judgments. There is no prohibition against appealing to regional human rights bodies, but there was no known case of an appeal. The legal system does not recognize the jurisdiction of the African Court on Human and Peoples' Rights.

f. Arbitrary or Unlawful Interference with Privacy, Family, Home, or Correspondence

The law prohibits such actions, and there were few reports the government failed to respect these provisions.

On May 11, the mayor of Andriampotsy village in Fenoarivobe District allegedly used his authority to prosecute a family for refusing to give him a portion of its inheritance.

On May 25, security forces confiscated the cell phone of Michel Ralibera, a journalist from Radio Antsiva, as he was covering the search of Senator Lylison's residence. Radio Antsiva intervened, accompanied by several government officials. The cell phone was returned to Ralibera after security forces reportedly searched all data on it.

Section 2. Respect for Civil Liberties, Including:

a. Freedom of Speech and Press

The constitution provides for freedom of speech and press, but these "may be limited by the respect for the freedoms and rights of others, and by the imperative of safeguarding public order, national dignity, and state security." The government restricted these rights more than in previous years. For example, the new communication code includes a number of provisions limiting freedom of speech and expression. The code also grants broad powers to the government to deny media licenses to political opponents, seize equipment, and impose fines.

The government also arrested opposition leaders who had called for protests around the country in response to foreign mining operations and land expropriation.

Freedom of Speech and Expression: Although the constitution provides for freedom of speech, the new communication code restricts such speech when it infringes on the freedoms or rights of others, endangers public order, or is believed to undermine national dignity or the security of the state. The new law restricts individuals' ability to criticize the government publicly.

Environmental activist Clovis Razafimalala has been imprisoned and awaiting trial since September 14 for his alleged incitement of violent demonstrations in Maroantsetra. Other activists claim he was jailed for his outspoken criticism of suspected rosewood trafficker Eric Besoa, a local power broker. His jailing was similar to the case of fellow activist Armand Marozafy, jailed for six months and fined 12 million ariary ($3,600) for defamation in 2015 when he sent a confidential report on illegal rosewood logging to NGO partners, subsequently posted on Facebook.

Press and Media Freedoms: The new communications code contains several articles limiting press and media freedoms.

For example, Article 85 requires the owner of a media company to be the chief publisher. This article may permit the harassment of potential opposition presidential candidates, many of whom were also media owners.

Although criminal defamation was eliminated from the communications code, a separate cyber criminality law allows for the charge of criminal defamation for anything published online. It was unclear whether the cyber criminality law, which includes prison sentences for online defamation, would have precedence over the new code, as all newspapers are also published online. The fines allowed for offenses under the new communications code are many times more than the average journalist's annual salary.

The new code gives the communications ministry far-reaching powers to suspend media licenses and seize property of media outlets if one of their journalists commits two infractions of the code. Finally, the new code allows only state-owned radio and television stations the right to broadcast nationally, although this limitation was not always enforced.

The country had numerous independent newspapers. More than 300 radio and television stations operated in the country, although many shifted to live call-in shows in recent years to distance themselves from editorial responsibility for content. Many of them continued to have a national audience, in spite of the legal limitations set by the new code. Nevertheless, limitations on private media existed. On May 12, Joel Ralaivaohita, vice president of the Association for CyberJournalists, stated that reporters were expected to reflect the views of media owners. He also stated that new television or radio channels could open only if they expressed political views supporting the government.

<u>Violence and Harassment</u>: On January 29, four individuals seriously beat Fernand Cello, a journalist working for Radio Jupiter. The journalist had been investigating an alleged organ trafficking ring in the south-central region. The previous week Cello had assisted security forces in the arrest of several persons suspected of involvement in organ trafficking.

On May 24, security force members beat Radio Antsiva journalist Michel Ralibera and confiscated his cell phone while they were conducting a search of Senator Lylison's residence. Ralibera was attempting to report on the search when the incident occurred.

On July 12, journalists were refused access to the National Assembly to cover the plenary session, open to the public, on the adoption of the communication code. Security force members who secured the area said they were acting on orders from the president of the National Assembly, who denied any involvement.

<u>Censorship or Content Restrictions</u>: Journalists practiced self-censorship, and authors generally published books of a political nature abroad.

The government often restricted or delayed licensing for media outlets critical of the government. For example, Radio MBS, owned by former president Marc Ravalomanana, filed a complaint with the State Council on March 12 to oppose the Ministry of Communications' decision to suspend its broadcasting license. Benjamin Rakotomandimby, the chief legal commissioner, stated that an investigation of the complaint would take six to nine months.

On March 23, security forces told journalists they were not permitted to take photographs or report on a car accident in Amborovy Mahajanga. The accident involved the minister of defense and occurred while he was on an official visit to the region. Security forces also reportedly threatened eyewitnesses speaking to journalists about the accident.

<u>Libel/Slander Laws</u>: There were several reports of government authorities using libel, slander, or defamation laws to restrict public discussion.

For example, on February 26, three journalists from the MaTV group were prosecuted for their reporting of the kidnapping of two minor siblings, Arland and Annie Ramiliarison. The journalists suggested the kidnapping was related to rosewood trafficking and alleged the kidnapped children's father was involved in the illegal trade. He sued them for defamation. The journalists also were accused of complicity in the kidnapping. On June 17, the court acquitted two of the journalists but sentenced the third to a 200,000 ariary ($60) fine, one million ariary ($300) in compensation for damages, and a one-month suspended sentence for defamation.

On May 25, authorities brought in Ndranto Razakamanarina, chairman of the NGO Alliance Voahary Gasy, to question him regarding defamation. The investigation was related to a press conference Razakamanarina held for his organization in January, in which he suggested government officials were involved in rosewood trafficking.

<u>National Security</u>: There were some reports of authorities using national security laws to restrict media distribution critical of the government.

On May 22, ARTEC, the communication regulation authority, threatened to shut down two privately owned radio stations, M3TV and Viva Radio. ARTEC stated their broadcasts interfered with frequencies used by ASECNA, the radio system used by the airports. Newspapers reported ARTEC's singling out these two channels for potential closure was due to their critical coverage of the government.

Internet Freedom

The government did not restrict or disrupt access to the internet, and there were no credible reports the government monitored private online communications without appropriate legal authority.

A 2014 cybercrime law prohibits insulting or defaming a government official online. According to Reporters Without Borders, "the law's failure to define what is meant by 'insult' or 'defamation' leaves room for very broad interpretation and major abuses." The law provides for punishment of two to five years' imprisonment and a fine of two million to 100 million ariary ($600 to $30,000) for defamation. Following criticism from the media and international community, the government promised to revise the law, but kept it unchanged in the new communications code.

Public access to the internet was limited mainly to urban areas. According to the International Telecommunication Union, 4.3 percent of the population used the internet in 2015.

Political groups, parties, and activists used the internet extensively to advance their agendas, share news, and criticize other parties. Observers generally considered the internet among the more reliable sources of information.

Academic Freedom and Cultural Events

There were no government restrictions on academic freedom or cultural events.

b. Freedom of Peaceful Assembly and Association

Freedom of Assembly

The constitution and law provide for freedom of assembly, but authorities restricted this right. Security forces regularly impeded opposition gatherings throughout the country and used excessive force to disperse demonstrators. They sometimes invoked legal procedures for unrelated crimes to dissuade protest leaders.

Several times during the year, security forces used tear gas to disperse demonstrations by university students and journalists in Antananarivo as well as protests in rural areas, such as Soamahamanina, where local residents had been protesting foreign mining operations for several months. Students generally retaliated by throwing stones at security forces, which often resulted in injuries and arrests.

Security forces were particularly active in restricting protests related to the communications code prior to its adoption by the legislature in July. For example, on July 13, security forces stopped a march in Antananarivo led by leaders of the Movement for Freedom of Expression. The march was billed as a "funeral for press freedom." Security forces also used tear gas on a group of demonstrators gathered by a monument to press freedom at the railway station in Analakely, in central Antananarivo.

On July 14, security forces imposed restrictions on the movement of residents of the rural commune of Soamahamanina after the local population protested the impact of Chinese mining operations on local tapia forests and associated traditional silk production. Gendarmes required all households to take down the protest banners they displayed on their walls, and those who refused had their banners confiscated. Later a group of villagers marched to the office of the commune to retrieve their confiscated banners, but security elements used tear gas and shot in the air to disperse the group. Protests continued at year's end.

Freedom of Association

The constitution and law provide for the right of association, but the government did not always respect this right. Opposition parties were regularly restricted from conducting public demonstrations.

c. Freedom of Religion

See the Department of State's *International Religious Freedom Report* at www.state.gov/religiousfreedomreport/.

d. Freedom of Movement, Internally Displaced Persons, Protection of Refugees, and Stateless Persons

The constitution and law provide for freedom of internal movement, foreign travel, emigration, and repatriation, and the government generally respected these rights. Authorities cooperated with the Office of the UN High Commissioner for Refugees (UNHCR) and other humanitarian agencies in providing protection and assistance to internally displaced persons, refugees, returning refugees, asylum seekers, stateless persons, and other persons of concern.

Protection of Refugees

<u>Access to Asylum</u>: The law does not include provisions for granting asylum or refugee status, but the government provides protection to refugees. Authorities cooperated with UNHCR and other humanitarian organizations in assisting the small number of refugees in the country.

Stateless Persons

A complicated system of citizenship laws and procedures resulted in a large number of stateless persons in the minority Muslim community, many belonging to families living in the country for generations. Muslim leaders estimated the laws affected as many as 5 percent of the approximately two million Muslims in the country.

Birth to a citizen parent transmits citizenship. Birth in the country does not automatically result in citizenship. Children born to a citizen mother and noncitizen father must declare their desire for citizenship by age 18 or risk losing eligibility for citizenship; the same applies to children born out of wedlock. Mothers confer nationality on children born in wedlock only if the father is stateless or of unknown nationality. Some members of the Karana community of Indo-Pakistani origin--who failed to register for Indian, Malagasy, or French citizenship following India's independence in 1947 and Madagascar's independence in 1960--were no longer eligible for any of the three citizenships; this circumstance applied to their descendants as well. Members of the wider Muslim community suggested a Muslim-sounding name alone could delay one's citizenship application indefinitely. All stateless persons may apply for a foreign resident card, which precludes the right to vote, own property, or apply for a passport, thus limiting international travel. Stateless women may obtain nationality by marrying a Malagasy citizen and may request citizenship before the wedding date. Stateless persons had difficulty accessing education and health care, could not get jobs or buy land, and lived in fear of arrest.

Section 3. Freedom to Participate in the Political Process

The constitution and law provide citizens the ability to choose their government in free and fair periodic elections held by secret ballot and based on universal and equal suffrage.

Elections and Political Participation

Recent Elections: The country held presidential and legislative elections in 2013. Despite irregularities that led to cancellation of results by the special electoral court (CES) in four districts, international observers--including the EU, African Union, Francophonie, and Carter Center--deemed the elections generally free and fair. In January 2014 the CES announced the official results, confirming Hery Rajaonarimampianina's election as president with 53 percent of the vote, compared with 47 percent for rival Jean-Louis Robinson. In the weeks that followed, the president appointed a prime minister and cabinet, and an elected National Assembly began its five-year term. The first session of the National Assembly in 2013 officially ended the five-year post-coup political transition.

On July 31, the country held municipal elections. They were marked by low turnout (25 percent) and irregularities, including exclusion of qualified voters from the polls, lack of independence of the independent election authority (CENI-T), cancellation of elections in 19 communes, and other problems.

In December 2015 the 12,664 mayors and municipal counsellors who were elected in July elected members of the Senate. The ruling HVM party won 36 of 42 seats after the High Constitutional Court rejected 11 complaints by opposition parties. The opposition cited undue influence by authorities on electors' votes in the senatorial contest and unequal financial resources available to candidates. The president appointed the remaining 21 senators.

Political Parties and Political Participation: The government restricted opposition parties and denied them their right to demonstrate spontaneously. Official permission is required for all demonstrations, and there were reports that the government denied or delayed permission for opposition parties, especially on national holidays or other symbolic dates.

<u>Participation of Women and Minorities</u>: No laws prevent women or members of minorities from voting, running for office, serving as election monitors, or otherwise participating in political life. Some observers believed that cultural and traditional factors prevented women from participating in political life on the same basis as men, however.

Section 4. Corruption and Lack of Transparency in Government

The law provides criminal penalties for official corruption, but the government did not implement the law effectively, and officials engaged in corrupt practices with impunity. Corruption was pervasive at all levels of government, and the World Bank's most recent worldwide governance indicators reflected corruption was a serious problem. There were numerous reports of government corruption during the year.

<u>Corruption</u>: The Independent Anticorruption Bureau (BIANCO) launched investigations on cases of corruption related to official exams to enter the gendarmerie school and the national school for penitentiary administration. The investigations revealed anomalies in the admission of new recruits but did not lead to any concrete prosecution of the officials involved.

There were no new developments in the effort to prosecute alleged rosewood kingpin Johnfrince Bekasy, launched by BIANCO in 2015. Bekasy, a candidate in the municipal elections for the president's party, remained free outside the country, having been released without explanation in October 2015.

In March 2014 a shipment of 30,000 rosewood logs was intercepted in Singapore, leading to a prosecution by Singapore, as the trade of rosewood is banned under the Convention on International Trade in Endangered Species of Wild Fauna and Flora (CITES). The Malagasy permit allowing export of the logs was issued in 2010, even though it contravened the CITES ban.

In 2015 the media reported on the case of the alleged misappropriation and embezzlement of 396 million ariary ($120,000) from the city of Ambohimasina by a businesswoman allegedly close to the president. Then prime minister Jean Ravelonarivo reportedly ordered the gendarmerie to arrest the accused businesswoman, but no action was taken. BIANCO opened an investigation into the allegation, but made no progress. The case was eventually transferred to the

Ministry of Justice, but insiders in the case stated the businesswoman's closeness to high-placed officials made any further development unlikely.

In 2015 BIANCO received 989 complaints involving corruption, of which 71 percent were judged eligible for investigation. The bureau referred 157 complaints for prosecution in 2015. The largest number of corruption complaints targeted the national gendarmerie, decentralized institutions, the education sector, the justice sector, and land management authorities. These cases, however, did not reflect the full extent of corruption in the country, as citizens were less likely to report larger scale corruption cases involving influential individuals.

Financial Disclosure: The law requires regular income and asset declaration for individuals in the following positions: prime minister and other government ministers; members of the National Assembly and Senate; members of the high constitutional court; chiefs of regions and mayors; magistrates; civil servants holding positions of or equivalent to ministry director and above; inspectors of land titling, treasury, tax, and finances; military officers at the company level and above; inspectors from the state general inspection, the army's general inspection, and the national gendarmerie's general inspection; and judicial police officers. Although BIANCO may inform the Prosecutor's Office in cases of noncompliance, there was no indication authorities applied sanctions for noncompliance.

Between January and September, 205 of 214 members of the National Assembly and Senate and all members of government required to do so, including the prime minister, declared their assets. As of December, 13 of the country's 22 heads of region had not declared their assets.

Public Access to Information: There are no laws providing for public access to government information.

Section 5. Governmental Attitude Regarding International and Nongovernmental Investigation of Alleged Violations of Human Rights

Numerous domestic and international human rights groups generally operated without restriction, investigating and publishing their findings on human rights cases. Government officials were not always responsive to their views, but authorities allowed international human rights groups to enter the country, conduct their work, and consult freely with other groups.

There were several domestic NGOs in the country that worked on human rights, but few had the capacity to work effectively and independently. Progovernment political organizations occasionally harassed or attempted to co-opt civil society groups.

Government Human Rights Bodies: In July 2014 the government established the legal framework for a national independent human rights commission composed of 11 commissioners, each elected by members of a different human rights organization and with a mandate to investigate cases and publish reports on human rights violations. By October 13, all 11 members of the commission had been sworn in, and the commission became publicly active. As of year's end, the government had not provided office space or funding for the commission.

Section 6. Discrimination, Societal Abuses, and Trafficking in Persons

Women

Rape and Domestic Violence: The law prohibits rape but does not address spousal rape. Penalties range from five years to life in prison, depending on factors such as the victim's age, the rapist's relationship to the victim, and whether the offender's occupation involved contact with children. Rape of a child or a pregnant woman is punishable by hard labor. Authorities may add an additional two to five years' imprisonment if the rape involves assault and battery. Authorities rarely enforced the law.

In 2015 the Vonjy Center at Befelatanana Public Hospital, Antananarivo, received 550 cases involving the rape of girls. Observers believed the figures greatly underestimated the extent of sexual violence nationwide, but no reliable national data were available. The UN Children's Fund (UNICEF) estimated that 14 percent of girls and young women between the ages of 15 and 19 in the country had experienced sexual violence.

The law prohibits domestic violence, but it remained a widespread problem. Domestic violence is punishable by two to five years in prison and a fine of four million ariary ($1,200), depending on the severity of injuries and whether the victim was pregnant. Statistics on the number of domestic abusers prosecuted, convicted, or punished were unavailable, but few women took legal action against their husbands, in part due to the 6,000 ariary ($1.80) cost of the required medical certificate. There were few shelters for battered women in the country, and many returned to the home of their parents, where parents often pressured them to return to their abusers.

Victims of domestic violence from vulnerable populations could receive assistance from advisory centers called Centers for Listening and Legal Advice (CECJ), set up in several regions by the Ministry of Population, Social Protection, and Promotion of Women with the support of the UN Population Fund (UNFPA). These centers counseled victims on where to go for medical care, provided psychological assistance, and helped them start legal procedures to receive alimony from their abusers.

During 2015 the CECJ received 1,103 cases of violence, 917 of which involved female victims of physical, economic, and moral domestic violence.

Sexual Harassment: Sexual harassment is against the law, and penalties range from one to three years' imprisonment and a fine of one to four million ariary ($300 to $1,200). The penalty increases to two to five years' imprisonment plus a fine of two to 10 million ariary ($600 to $3,000) if criminals forced or pressured the victim into sexual acts or punished the victim for refusing such advances. Authorities did not enforce the law, and sexual harassment was widespread.

In July the morality and minor protection unit within the national police, in partnership with UNICEF and a Malagasy telecommunications company, took part in training on prevention of internet-based sexual harassment for dozens of children between the ages of 13 and 18.

Reproductive Rights: Couples and individuals who are 18 and older have the right to decide the number, spacing, and timing of children, free from discrimination, coercion, or violence, but they often lacked the information and means to do so.

According to the World Health Organization, the maternal mortality ratio was 353 maternal deaths per 100,000 live births. Major factors that contributed to high maternal mortality included the distance from and high cost of health centers, low quality of hospital services, chronic maternal malnutrition (including anemia), lack of adequate spacing between pregnancies, and the high rate of unsafe abortions. Although marriage under the age of 18 is prohibited except in extreme circumstances, and then only with concurrence of both parents and legal authorities, both marriage and pregnancy under the age of 18 were common. Persons under the age of 18, even if married, are not legally allowed to obtain birth control.

The UNFPA estimated 36.4 percent of women and girls between the ages of 15 and 49 used a modern method of contraception in 2015. Observers estimated skilled attendance during childbirth at 44 percent, but lower in rural areas, where there were few trained health workers.

Public health clinics provided free contraceptives and family planning information to adults, but such services often were unavailable due to inadequate resources. Religious organizations, NGO clinics, and other private sector organizations provided such services. Social and cultural barriers as well as resource problems also impeded the use of contraceptives.

In April the Ministry of Education signed a partnership with Population Service International to increase understanding of reproductive health for girls in public schools across the country.

Discrimination: While women enjoyed the same legal status and rights as men in some areas, there were significant differences. Women experienced discrimination in employment, transfer of nationality to their children, and inheritance. While widows with children inherit half of joint marital property, a husband's surviving kin have priority over widows without children, leaving the widow eighth in line for inheritance if there is no prior agreement. Families did not always observe these provisions. A tradition known as "the customary third" provides the wife with the right to only one-third of a couple's joint holdings upon dissolution of the marriage, and families occasionally observed this tradition.

A number of NGOs focused on the civic education of women and girls, publicizing and explaining legal protections for women. Illiteracy, cultural traditions, societal intimidation, and lack of knowledge prevented many women from lodging official complaints or seeking redress when authorities violated their rights.

Children

Birth Registration: Citizenship derives from one's parents, although children born to a citizen mother and a foreign father must declare their desire for citizenship by age 18. Mothers may confer nationality on children born in wedlock only if the father is stateless or of unknown nationality. The country had no uniformly enforced birth registration system, and unregistered children typically were not eligible to attend school or obtain health-care services. UNICEF worked with the government to provide birth certificates for newborn children and children who did not receive a certificate at birth. According to a 2010 UNICEF study, 80 percent of children under the age of five had their births registered. The Ministries of Interior, Health, and Justice worked with UNICEF to reduce the number of unregistered children in targeted regions.

Education: The constitution provides for tuition-free public education for all citizen children and makes primary education until the age of 16 compulsory. Nevertheless, parents were increasingly required to pay various registration and other fees to subsidize teacher salaries and other costs. As a result, education became inaccessible for many children. According to UNICEF, boys and girls generally had equal access to education, although girls were more likely to drop out during adolescence. Beginning in 2014, the World Bank supported a three-year project, carried out by the Ministry of Population, to provide financial support to families to improve access to education. The program was intended to cover 39,000 families in several regions and provide money to vulnerable families in exchange for a commitment to send their children to school.

Child Abuse: Child abuse was a problem, including the rape of babies and toddlers. The press reported more than 15 cases of child rape, with most victims under the age of 12; the youngest was three years old. During 2015 the Union of Social Workers dealt with 40 cases of child abuse involving victims between the ages of three months and 18 years. In 2015, drawing on data from the national police and the Ministry of Population, UNICEF reported 417 cases of rape and 828 other cases of child abuse. Government efforts to combat child rape were limited, focusing primarily on child protection networks, which addressed the needs of victims and helped raise public awareness.

The Vonjy Center, in the maternity wing of Befelatanana Public Hospital, continued to operate. Funded by UNICEF, the center received and treated minors who were victims of rape. The center also offered medical consultation, coverage of medical expenses and delivery in case of pregnancy, treatment for the psychological impact of rape, and support from the Morality and Minor Police to record complaints. The center encouraged victims to persuade their parents to file charges against perpetrators.

Early and Forced Marriage: The legal age for marriage without parental consent is 18 for both boys and girls. Nevertheless, according to UNFPA, child marriage remained very common, particularly in rural areas and in the south. An estimated 41 percent of women between the ages of 20 and 24 were married before 18, and 12 percent were married before 15, according to UNICEF surveys in 2008-14.

As confirmed by the UN special rapporteur on modern forms of slavery during her mission to the country in 2012, early forced marriage remained a concern in many communities, where parents forced girls as young as 10 to marry. She noted that victims of such arrangements were also likely to be victims of domestic servitude and sexual slavery.

According to a 2013 report by the UN special rapporteur, the practice of "moletry," in which girls are married off at a younger age in exchange for oxen received as a dowry, continued. The parents of a boy (usually around age 15) look for a spouse for their son (girls may be as young as 12), after which the parents of both children organize the wedding. The parents hold a written agreement for one year that they may prolong. If a child is born after the first year and the marriage contract has expired, the girl--or, if she is very young, her mother--will be responsible for raising the child. If the girl has been unfaithful or the marriage does not last the full year, parents return the dowry, without any stigma for either side. The wife must stay the contracted year, even in the case of domestic violence, in which case the girl's parents receive more money or jewels.

The UN special rapporteur also criticized the practice of "valifofo," or arranged marriage. She noted in places like Ihorombe, in the Bara community, when a girl reaches the age of 10, she is separated from other family members and may receive male visitors without obtaining approval from her male relatives. In the Bara community, the parents betroth a girl at birth, and the parents receive 10 oxen. The man may take the girl at age seven or ask her parents to raise her until she is age 12, at which time parents take her to the husband's home.

Sexual Exploitation of Children: The recruitment and incitement to prostitution generally carries a penalty of two to five years' imprisonment and a fine of up to 10 million ariary ($3,000). Antitrafficking legislation, however, provides a penalty of forced labor for the recruitment and incitement to prostitution involving a child under the age of 18, the sexual exploitation of a child under 15, and the commercial exploitation of a child under 18. Both the penal code and antitrafficking laws address pornography, specifying penalties of two to five years' imprisonment and fines up to 10 million ariary ($3,000). Authorities rarely enforced the provisions. There is no minimum legal age for consensual sex.

The sexual exploitation of children, sometimes with the involvement of parents, remained a significant problem. The problem was particularly acute in Antananarivo and coastal cities, including Toamasina, Nosy Be, Diego Suarez, and

Mahajanga. During her 2013 mission, the UN special rapporteur called the "exponential growth" of child prostitution and sex tourism in the country "alarming."

In 2013, in the latest report available, the NGO Ending Child Prostitution and Trafficking in Madagascar documented 1,132 children in prostitution in Antananarivo; more than one third claimed to have been initiated into prostitution during the previous year. The NGO also reported criminals initiated most children in prostitution in the coastal cities of Mahajanga and Nosy Be at between the ages of 13 and 15. In 40 percent of the cases, the children had their first sexual encounter as sex workers, and their parents often were aware of their activities.

Employers often abused and raped young rural girls working as housekeepers in the capital. If they left their work, employers typically did not pay them, so many remained rather than return empty-handed to their families and villages.

The Ministry of Population operated approximately 450 multisector networks covering 22 regions throughout the country to protect children from abuse and exploitation. The ministry collaborated with UNICEF to identify child victims and provide for their access to adequate medical and psychosocial services. In collaboration with the gendarmerie, the Ministry of Justice, and the Ministry of Population, UNICEF trained local law enforcement officials and other stakeholders in targeted regions on the rights of children.

Several cultural and traditional practices resulted in the sexual exploitation of young women and girls. For example, in some remote areas, the traditional practice of "Tsenan'ampela" (girl markets) continued. Starting at age 13, girls go to cattle markets, where they try to attract cattle owners and negotiate a price for a "marriage," which can last for a night or the duration of the market (from Friday to Monday), according to the UN special rapporteur's 2013 report. Such girls generally were paid up to 10,000 ariary ($3) a night and returned home after the market.

Infanticide or Infanticide of Children with Disabilities: Media reports documented several deaths of newborns abandoned in gutters and dumpsters. A traditional taboo in the southeast against giving birth to twins also contributed to the problem.

Displaced Children: Although child abandonment is against the law, it remained a significant problem. There were few safe shelters for street children, and governmental agencies generally tried first to place abandoned children with parents or other relatives. Authorities placed many children in private and church-affiliated orphanages outside the regulated system.

International Child Abductions: The country is a party to the 1980 Hague Convention on the Civil Aspects of International Child Abduction. See the Department of State's *Annual Report on International Parental Child Abduction* at travel.state.gov/content/childabduction/english/legal/compliance.html.

Anti-Semitism

The Jewish community was small, and there were no reports of anti-Semitic acts.

Trafficking in Persons

See the Department of State's *Trafficking in Persons Report* at www.state.gov/j/tip/rls/tiprpt/.

Persons with Disabilities

The law prohibits discrimination against persons with physical and mental disabilities, although there is no specific mention of sensory and intellectual disabilities. The law broadly defines the rights of persons with disabilities and provides for a national commission and regional sub-commissions to promote their rights. By law persons with disabilities are entitled to receive health care and education and have the right to training and employment; the law does not address air travel or access to the judicial system. Educational institutions are "encouraged" to make necessary infrastructure adjustments to accommodate students with disabilities. The law also specifies the state "must facilitate, to the extent possible, access to its facilities, public spaces, and public transportation to accommodate persons with disabilities."

Authorities rarely enforced the rights of persons with disabilities, and the legal framework for promoting accessibility remained perfunctory. According to a comprehensive study commissioned by a local NGO, in addition to excluding the specific rights of women and children with disabilities, the legal framework covering disabilities lacks key themes, such as accessibility, autonomy, personal mobility, equality, access to justice, the ability to participate in public life and politics.

Access to education and health care for persons with disabilities also was limited due to lack of adequate infrastructure, specialized institutions, and personnel. Nevertheless, disability advocates reported there were more than 60 integrated classrooms across the country that included children with mental disabilities. Local officials also accommodated students with sensory disabilities during official high school examinations. With the financial support of a French organization, the minister of education signed an agreement with Handicap International in February for the inclusion of 2,173 vulnerable children, including 503 children with disabilities, into the public schools in the regions of Diana and Analanjirofo. The program included specialized training for teachers from primary public schools to receive those children.

Persons with disabilities encountered discrimination in employment. They were also were more likely to become victims of abuse, sometimes perpetrated by their own relatives. For example, the leader of an association of women with disabilities reported in 2015 that two of their members had forcible tubal ligations ordered by their parents to prevent them from having more children, since the parents considered them burdens on their families.

The electoral code provides that individuals with disabilities be assisted in casting their ballots, but it contains no other provisions to accommodate voters with disabilities.

The Ministry of Population is responsible for protecting the rights of persons with disabilities and includes a directorate in charge of persons with disabilities and elderly persons. The ministry appointed a woman with disabilities to lead the directorate.

In partnership with Handicap International, local governments also participated in an inclusive communal development program. The communes of Toamasina and Toliara significantly improved the accessibility of markets and other public places for persons with disabilities.

The Ministry of Population announced a five-year national inclusion plan on disability in 2015. The plan was to serve as a toolkit for all public and private actors and entities to include disability rights in their respective programs.

National/Racial/Ethnic Minorities

None of the 18 tribes in the country constituted a majority. There were also minorities of Indo-Pakistani, Comorian, and Chinese heritage. Ethnicity, caste, and regional solidarity often were considered in hiring and exploited in politics. A long history of military conquest and political dominance by highland ethnic groups of Asian origin, particularly the Merina, over coastal groups of African ancestry contributed to tension between citizens of highland and coastal descent, particularly in politics.

Acts of Violence, Discrimination, and Other Abuses Based on Sexual Orientation and Gender Identity

The law provides for a prison sentence of two to five years and a fine of two to 10 million ariary ($600 to $3,000) for acts that are "indecent or against nature with an individual of the same sex under the age of 21," which is understood to include all sexual relations. There is no law prohibiting same-sex sexual conduct for those over age 21. Members of the lesbian, gay, bisexual, transgender, and intersex (LGBTI) community reportedly were unaware of the risk of arrest for "corruption of a minor," and arrests occurred, although there were no official statistics. There are no specific antidiscrimination provisions that apply to LGBTI persons. No laws prevent transgender persons from identifying with their chosen gender.

There were reports of official discrimination and that local officials, particularly law enforcement personnel, either abused LGBTI persons or failed to protect them from societal violence. Health officials also reportedly denied services to LGBTI persons or failed to respect confidentiality agreements.

Sexual orientation and gender identity were not widely discussed, with public attitudes ranging from tacit acceptance to violent rejection, particularly of transgender sex workers. Members of this community faced considerable social stigma and discrimination, often within their own families and particularly in rural areas. Relatives ostracized many and refused them burial in the family tomb. LGBTI individuals often faced discrimination in hiring.

HIV and AIDS Social Stigma

Providers in the health-care sector subjected persons with HIV/AIDS to stigma and discrimination. HIV/AIDS patients have the right to free health care, and the law specifies sanctions against persons who discriminate against or marginalize persons with HIV/AIDS. Apart from the National Committee for the Fight against

AIDS in Madagascar, national institutions--including the Ministries of Health and Justice--did not effectively enforce the law.

Other Societal Violence or Discrimination

Mob violence occurred in both urban and rural areas, in large part due to crime and lack of public confidence in police and the judiciary. Crowds killed, beat, burned, or otherwise injured suspected criminals or accomplices, and the media reported 86 mob killings between January and December. Authorities sometimes arrested the perpetrators, but fear of creating renewed anger hindered effectiveness of the prosecution.

On March 1, in Maroantsetra, gendarmes arrested a cattle owner for allegedly having taken part in a mob killing of a cattle rustler in November 2014. In response, on March 3, a group of angry villagers assaulted and sacked the prosecutor's office and began marching to the prison to release the imprisoned cattle owner. To avoid a prison break, the local magistrate issued an order to release him.

On March 31, an angry mob in Bealanana beat to death two alleged thieves, who had been arrested by gendarmes, and cut their dead bodies into pieces.

Persons with albinism in the country also suffer witchcraft-related attacks. For example, on October 17, the body of a 28-year-old woman with albinism was found in Betioky, in the south, with the eyes removed. In November a priest with albinism who escaped kidnappers reported they had intended to sell him for 60 million ariary ($18,000), presumably so his body parts could be used in witchcraft.

Section 7. Worker Rights

a. Freedom of Association and the Right to Collective Bargaining

The law provides that public and private sector workers may establish and join labor unions of their choice without prior authorization or excessive requirements. Civil servants and maritime workers have separate labor codes. Essential workers--including police, military, and firefighters--may not form unions. The maritime code, which governs workers in the maritime sector, does not specifically provide the right to form unions.

The law generally allows for union activities and provides most workers the right to strike, including workers in export processing zones (EPZs). Authorities prohibit strikes, however, if there is a possibility of "disruption of public order" or if the strike would endanger the life, safety, or health of the population. Workers must first exhaust conciliation, mediation, and compulsory arbitration remedies, which may take eight months to two and a half years. Magistrates and workers in other "essential services" (not defined by law) have a recognized but more restricted right to strike. The law requires them to maintain a basic level of service and to give prior notice to their employer. The labor code also provides for a fine, imprisonment, or both for the "instigators and leaders of illegal strikes," even if the strike is peaceful.

The law prohibits antiunion discrimination by employers. In the event of antiunion activity, unions or their members may file suit against the employer in civil court. The law does not accord civil servants and public sector employees legal protection against antiunion discrimination and interference. The labor code does not address reinstatement of workers fired for union activity.

The law provides workers in the private sector, except for seafarers, the right to bargain collectively. Public sector employees not engaged in the administration of the state, such as teachers hired under the auspices of donor organizations or parent associations in public schools, do not have the right to bargain collectively. According to union representatives, authorities did not always enforce applicable laws, including effective remedies and penalties, and procedures were subject to lengthy delays and appeals. Larger international firms, such as in the telecommunications and banking sectors, more readily exercised and respected collective bargaining rights. These rights, however, were reportedly more difficult to exercise in EPZs and smaller local companies. Union representatives reported workers in such companies often were reluctant to make demands due to fear of reprisal.

The government generally respected freedom of association and collective bargaining. The law provides that unions operate independently from the government and political parties. Union representatives indicated there were subtle attempts by employers to dissuade or influence unions, which often prevented workers from organizing or criticizing poor working conditions.

Strikes occurred throughout the year, including by universities, public school teachers, court clerks, and customs office employees. These movements were not always related to labor conditions, and some officials suggested strikers intended such actions to "destabilize" the country. The government sometimes resorted to various forms of harassment to intimidate movement leaders, sometimes using unrelated charges.

On the occasion of Labor Day on May 1, an association of labor unions named "Afo Sendikaly" held a public gathering in Antananarivo in which a number of speakers, including well-known figures from the political opposition, criticized the government. Several days later, during another meeting, the leaders of the association gave a 72-hour ultimatum to the president to resign. On June 6, Maharavo Ratolojanahary, one of the leaders, announced he had received a letter of reprimand signed by the prime minister, who was also the minister of interior, accusing him of disciplinary offenses and reminding him he did not have authorization to speak on behalf of the civil administrators' union.

On May 2, Tsinjo Rakotomaharo, a physician in the public administration, was notified of his dismissal at the recommendation of a disciplinary board for dereliction of duty by taking part in a labor union activity. Rakotomaharo alleged that his dismissal, approved by the prime minister, was a form of revenge for having criticized the territorial rearrangement of Antananarivo when the prime minister had been minister of the interior and decentralization. Rakotomaharo was also an active member of the opposition TIM political party.

The EPZ law restricted worker rights by allowing labor laws in EPZs to vary from the country's standard labor code. EPZ labor contracts may differ in terms of contract duration, restrictions on the employment of women during night shifts, and the amount of overtime permitted. This law initially authorized women to work during night shifts not exceeding six hours per week. The decree of enforcement adopted in 2015, however, provides that employers require the personal consent of the worker and that before introducing night shifts for women, companies must consult with labor unions to identify the most appropriate conditions.

b. Prohibition of Forced or Compulsory Labor

The law prohibits forced labor, but it was a significant problem among children in the informal sector. Forced labor also persisted in the context of "dinas," informal arrangements for payment or in response to wrongdoing (see section 1.d.). In some communities dinas were an accepted way of resolving conflicts or paying debt. These arrangements persisted because authorities did not effectively enforce the law. In 2014 the legislature adopted antitrafficking legislation with associated penalties, which provides a broader definition of trafficking (to include forced labor).

Also see the Department of State's *Trafficking in Persons Report* at www.state.gov/j/tip/rls/tiprpt/.

c. Prohibition of Child Labor and Minimum Age for Employment

The law regulates working conditions of children, defines the worst forms of child labor, identifies penalties for employers, and establishes the institutional framework for implementation. The legal minimum age for employment is 15. The law allows children to work a maximum of eight hours per day and 40 hours per week with no overtime, and it prohibits persons under the age of 18 from working at night and at sites where there is an imminent danger to health, safety, or morals. Employers must observe a mandatory 12-hour rest period between shifts. Occupational health and safety regulations include requirements for parental authorization and a medical examination before hiring. The law prohibits hazardous occupations and activities for children but does not prohibit hazardous occupations and activities in all relevant child labor sectors, including agriculture.

The government did not effectively enforce the law. The Ministry of Civil Services and Administrative Reform is responsible for enforcing child labor laws. It also operated the Manjarisoa Center in Antananarivo, which offered services to 35 victims of exploitative child labor in 2015, the latest figure available. Although labor inspectors were generalists, they received training on child labor and could conduct child labor inspections; however, they did not operate in the large informal sector where child labor occurred.

During the year the Directorate of Labor within the Ministry of Civil Services and Administrative Reform appointed a dozen labor inspectors specifically to cover child labor issues. The mission of the newly appointed inspectors was to identify and report the forms of child labor, including the worst forms, prevailing within their respective regions. They were also entitled to conduct sensitization and site visits.

Child labor was a widespread problem. Centers operated by NGOs in Antananarivo, Toamasina, and Toliara received children, including victims of trafficking and forced labor. Children in rural areas worked mostly in agriculture, fishing, and livestock herding, while those in urban areas worked in domestic labor, transport of goods by rickshaw, petty trading, stone quarrying, artisanal mining for gemstones such as sapphires, bars, and as beggars. Children also worked in the vanilla sector, salt production, deep-sea diving, and the shrimp industry. Some children were trafficked internally for purposes of forced labor, including child prostitution.

Also see the Department of Labor's *Findings on the Worst Forms of Child Labor* at www.dol.gov/ilab/reports/child-labor/findings/.

d. Discrimination with Respect to Employment and Occupation

Labor laws prohibit discrimination based on race, gender, religion, political opinion, origin, and disability in the workplace. A special decree related to HIV in the workplace addresses prohibition of discrimination based on serology status. The law does not prohibit discrimination based on sexual orientation, gender identity, age, or language. Discrimination remained a problem. Employers subjected persons with disabilities and LGBTI individuals to hiring discrimination.

There was little societal discrimination against women in urban areas, where many women owned or managed businesses and held management positions in private businesses or state-owned companies. In rural areas, however, where most of the population engaged in subsistence farming, traditional social structures tended to favor entrenched gender roles. While there was little discrimination in access to employment and credit, women often did not receive equal pay for substantially similar work. Employers did not permit women to work in positions that might endanger their health, safety, or morals. According to the labor and social protection codes, such positions included night shifts in the manufacturing sector and certain positions in the mining, metallurgy, and chemical industries. During the country's latest universal periodic review in 2014, officials reported the government increased inspectors to overcome gaps in the verification system regarding discrimination against women and worked to promote equal employment opportunities in the EPZs.

e. Acceptable Conditions of Work

On February 17, the government raised the monthly minimum wage to 144,003 ariary ($43) for nonagricultural workers and 146,060 ariary ($44) for agricultural workers. The official government estimate for the poverty income level was 47,900 ariary ($14.40) per month.

The standard workweek was 40 hours in nonagricultural and service industries and 42.5 hours in the agricultural sector. The law limits workers to 20 hours of overtime per week and requires 2.5 days of paid annual leave per month. If the hours worked exceed the legal limits for working hours (2,200 hours per year in agriculture and 173.33 hours per month in other sectors), employers are legally required to pay overtime in accordance with a labor council decree, which also denotes the required amount of overtime pay. If more than five hours of overtime are required in addition to the regular 40-hour workweek, employers must request authorization from a labor inspector before imposing the additional overtime. Overtime may not exceed 20 hours per week. The law applies to all workers, although it is the responsibility of the labor inspector to define the kind of work a worker may perform under such an authorization.

The government sets occupational safety and health standards for workers and workplaces, but the labor code does not define penalties for noncompliance, which only requires an inspection before a company may open. Workers, including foreign or migrant workers, have an explicit right to leave a dangerous workplace without jeopardizing their employment as long as they inform their supervisors. Labor activists noted that standards, dating to the country's independence in some cases, were severely outdated, particularly regarding health and occupational hazards, and classification of professional positions. There was no enforcement in the large informal sector.

A 2015 study of the garment and leather industry conducted by the Friedrich Ebert Stiftung (FES), a German foundation, revealed that all 126 companies investigated in Antananarivo had set up safety systems, such as fire extinguishers and emergency exits, but that only 11 percent of them provided individual protection equipment to workers. The same study reported that 40 percent of employees from the investigated companies, along with their families, were deprived of basic social services because a significant number of employers failed to pay contributions to the national fund for social welfare since the 2009-13 political crisis.

The Ministry of Civil Services and Administrative Reform is responsible for enforcing minimum wage and working conditions, but this did not always occur. The ministry, which had approximately 130 labor inspectors on the ground and another 10 in training, had only enough inspectors to monitor conditions in the capital, although it continued to train more in partnership with the International Labor Organization. The national fund for social welfare, the country's social security agency, conducted inspections and published reports on workplace conditions, occupational health hazards, and workplace accident trends. Apart from increasing the minimum wage and conducting an insufficient number of inspections, authorities reportedly took no other action during the year to prevent violations and improve working conditions.

Violations of wage, overtime, or occupational safety and health standards were common in the informal sector and in domestic work, where many worked long hours for less than minimum wage. Although most employees knew the legal minimum wage, employers did not always pay those rates. High unemployment and widespread poverty led workers to accept lower wages. Employers often required employees to work until they met production targets. In some cases this overtime was unrecorded and unpaid. Employers did not always respect the right to remove oneself from a dangerous workplace.

EPZ companies generally respected labor laws, as many foreign importers required good working conditions in compliance with local law before signing contracts with EPZ companies. Labor organizations, however, reported a shift in recent years from paying hourly wages to a piece rate payment system that negatively affected the conditions of laborers in the textile sector, who primarily were female. The practice, designed to increase productivity, reportedly led to an increase in work-related accidents and negatively affected the health of women. Observers declared many women unsuitable to occupy these positions by age 40. The FES reported in its 2015 study that EPZ companies prioritized setting a production target that was generally difficult to attain, penalizing workers under various forms of sanctions, such as unpaid overtime, disciplinary sanctions, or even dismissal.